HAVE YOUR HAPPINESS

A short guide to owning your happiness and being rich in "happy currency."

Copyright © 2020 Julian Bernard Jelks Jr
All rights reserved. This book or any portion thereof
may not be reproduced or used in any manner whatsoever
without the express written permission of the publisher
except for the use of brief quotations in a book review.

Printed in the United States of America

First Printing, 2021

Published by 1888 House LLC
10 Glenlake Pkwy,
Suite 130, Atlanta, GA
30328

ISBN 978-1-7373645-0-4

HAVE YOUR HAPPINESS

A short guide to owning your happiness and being rich in "happy currency."

J.B. WATERS

Contents

***Preface**:*
Does the World Control Our Happiness?
v

***Introduction**:*
The Gift of Happiness.
vii

Part I. What Is Happiness to You?
1

Part II. High on Happiness
10

Part III. Own Your Happy
19

Part IV. Rich in Happiness
28

Part V. Speak Happiness, Hear Happiness
(Affirmations, Quotes and Mantras)
35

Conclusion
Your Happiness Is Yours.
42

Blank Space for Notes
44

PREFACE

I am not happy. This does not make me happy. You are not making me happy. You make me so happy. These are all statements made by everyone at some point in their life. Each one of these statements shares one similarity. Can you identify what it is? Let me save you the time and headache. All of these statements recognize happiness as something that has to be made or created outside of self rather than something that comes from within. What is it that makes people believe we must acquire or possess a thing before we can feel the reward of happiness? What is it that makes people feel a lack of happiness when certain people or things are absent? Is it that we humans have not dug in the right area to find the treasure of truth in this matter that we seek?

The burden of finding consistent happiness has weighed heavily on the hearts and minds of all who have felt this void. At the end of every action or aspiration is the finish line of happiness. People search the earth high and wide trying to find something that they've possessed since the very beginning. This misconception of placing happiness outside of your own mind and heart has plagued us since the days of antiquity. Men and women have written hundreds of thousands of words in manuscripts trying to solve the issue of suffering and sadness and its relativity to happiness within the heart and mind of mankind. Our emotional state as human beings relies heavily on what we believe makes us happy or feel fulfilled in our lives. Imagine a life where you no longer have to be with someone or acquire something to have that overwhelming feeling of happiness. A life where you can turn on your happiness with the same ease as flipping a light switch.

I aspire to bring light and resolution to this matter with the contents explained in this guide. In the back of this guide are blank pages for you to write any ideas, items or information that may be requested of you. This information will be helpful to you as a reference point throughout your journey on becoming rich in "happy currency". There will also be blank lines in throughout the guide that will allow you to jot your thoughts immediately. When you complete this guide you will be on the path that will lead you to the treasure of truth you long for. The truth that your happiness belongs to you and is all the richest you will ever need.

INTRODUCTION

   The multicolored lights shine bright on the tree with gifts wrapped tightly, while the stockings hang over the fireplace nearby. Knowing that you are anxiously waiting, Mother tries to keep you occupied with cookies decorated like snowmen and Christmas trees. As Christmas morning approaches you can't help but to fight your sleep by singing all the Christmas songs you've been hearing all holiday season. You begin to feel yourself slowly go into a place of wonder, thinking of all the possibilities of gifts you may receive this year. Shoes, toys, that game console you've been dying to have.... What could it be? The more you mentally stroll through your list of gifts, your excitement starts to give you a level of happiness as if you've already received them. You begin to picture yourself ripping through the wrapping paper and trying on those new shoes you've been begging for all year. You start to see yourself playing outside with that brand new Nerf gun that you've been wanting but didn't receive for your birthday.

   With too much excitement to hold in, you run to your mother and ask her if you can open just one gift tonight. Pleased by your discipline and patience, she allows you to open one gift before morning. As you look over the gifts under the tree, you find yourself more and more excited about what each box may contain. Not allowing another second to pass, you choose a box with your name on it and begin to rip the paper off. While opening the box you slowly notice hints of what may be confined inside. Finally getting through the neatly wrapped Christmas paper, you realize that you've opened the box you wanted the most. To your surprise, inside the box is the game console that you wanted more than any other gift. With the joy you had prior to opening the gift paired with the new feeling of knowing you got exactly what you wanted, you become filled with an overwhelming amount of happiness.

This event will be locked in your childhood memories for years to come, and it will be remembered as a time when you felt happy due to a certain event in your life. This event will always be a memory that will bring you into a state of happiness, no matter what you're going through. In our lives we will have several moments like the one we just read. There will be times in our lives where we will relate our level of happiness to certain events. And on the flipside, there will be times when we relate some form of sadness and pain to other events.

As you recall those times in your life that you relate to happiness, I want you to think of how you felt prior to whatever happened that made you feel happy. Do you remember if you were happy before the event? If you received an item, can you recall if you were excited beforehand? Once we really take a look at our past events and how they made us feel, we begin to notice that during times when we had expectations that certain events would happen or that we would receive certain items, there were feelings that existed within us. We felt a certain level of happiness prior to the events themselves. As we noticed with the story of the child on Christmas Eve, the thought of receiving something produced a level of happiness comparable to, if not more than, the act of receiving the item itself. So, the question is, does the happiness we feel lie in the items we receive or events that happen in our lives, or is it something that we already possess within us? In this short guide "Have Your Happiness", you will learn how to own your happiness and find how to adjust your level of happiness at will. You will see that all you desire is only a catalyst that can assist you in summoning the happiness that you must already have inside. This guide will be an everyday reference to give you the tools you'll need to find where your happiness should come from, how to remain rich in happiness no matter the external circumstance and give you the proper steps to maintain ownership of your happiness at all times.

In today's society we are told that you cannot give or use something and keep it as your own. The world says you can't give your time, love and happiness and still have it remain with you. In other words, you can't have your cake and eat it too. Well, I am here to tell you that if you can't have your cake and eat it too, you can "Have Your Happiness" and eat it too.

Part I

1. What Is Happiness to You?

Basis:
- Define what happiness means to you.
- List the things, actions or people that you relate to happiness.
- Identify your reasoning or logic behind why you relate these things to a feeling of happiness.
- Learn how to detach from the items that you believe bring you happiness.
-Implement regimens that will assist you in learning how to find happiness in the absence of the items listed.

IDEOLOGY

Happiness means something different to everyone. Some people describe happiness as a feeling that they have inside. Some people relate happiness to an object or person they know. The idea of what happiness is varies from person to person. The purpose of this part to having your happiness is to identify what you as an individual feel, think or believes happiness means to you. You must first recognize what happiness is to you personally before you can fully understand if what you are missing is essential to it.

Being able to relate your perspective to your desires is key to finding the issue and/or solution to the problems you face in terms of happiness. The tricky part of not knowing what you want is the fact you may deny or reject what you need in your life because you don't know exactly what you're looking for. People often find themselves lost and stuck, not knowing what they want, because they don't spend enough time doing self-analysis. It takes a true love for your own character flaws and weaknesses to be compelled to analyze yourself. What people consider to be a source of their happiness will tell you a lot about what is important to them. We tend to put energy into what we care about the most. So, whatever it is you care about the most will be the thing that has the ability to control your happiness. That's why it's of utmost importance to identify what you have the strongest emotional and mental connection to. In order to have your happiness, you must focus your energy in the right direction. Happiness is literally whatever you allow it to be at face value. How you view your life with or without the perceived basis of your happiness will determine how much control you have over your own happiness.

Step 1: What Is Happiness to You?

- Identify the things, actions or people that you relate the feeling of happiness to.

_____

_____

_____

_____

_____

* Purpose: Knowing this will give you a better idea of how to identify with happiness, joy and pleasure. Knowing exactly what gives you happiness is the first step to claiming and owning your happiness.

- Place items and relationships on a list from 1-10 based on the level of happiness you think each item makes you feel.

_____

_____

_____

_____

_____

_____

_____

_____

_____

* Purpose: Writing the items down in a list will help you realize the power or lack thereof in each item by seeing them ranked visually. It will also give you a chance to weigh the true value that each item has on your overall happiness.

- Why do you relate these things with happiness?

_____

_____

_____

_____

* Purpose: By knowing your reasoning for relating these things to happiness, you can have a more in-depth idea of the meaning behind your attachment to them. This will help you figure out if there is an underlying cause for your attachment to each item.

-Did you consider yourself to be happy before you had these things or knew these people?

_____

_____

_____

_____

_____

* Purpose: Being aware of your previous level of happiness before you acquired those relationships or things allows you to be conscious of how much effect these things really have your level of happiness. Once you become aware of this, you will notice that your level of happiness was not related to the acquisition of the item or relationship but more to the feeling you experienced prior to obtaining them.

PLAN OF ACTION:

1.Deny yourself anyone or any activity that gives you the feeling of happiness.

Step 1: Five minutes

Step 2: One hour

Step 3: One day

-AFTER REMOVING THESE ITEMS FROM YOUR LIFE, RECORD ANY CHANGES IN LEVEL OF HAPPINESS FROM 1-10. **(ON EACH LINE WRITE THE DAY, DURATION, AND HAPPINESS LEVEL)**

_____

_____

_____

_____

_____

2. Concentrate on how long this feeling of happiness last during or after you possess this thing or engage these people.

*Record the amount of time you are having these feelings.

_____

_____

_____

_____

3. Do you consider your happiness to be attached only to these items or ideas? Have you felt happiness in the absence of these things or ideas? Write down all the items and list how you felt prior to and after the acquisition of these items and relationships.

_____

_____

_____

Keys to Remember: What Is Happiness to You?

- Whatever you identify as the source of your happiness is what will most likely control your mental, physical and emotional state.

- Always be aware of why you may feel something is the cause of your happiness.

- Remember to analyze if a person, thing or place is the reason your level of happiness is changing in that moment, just for the sake of noticing how you felt prior to the acquisition of that relationship, place or thing.

- Knowing how long something gives you the feeling of happiness will help you gauge how much emotional connection you have to it.

- Take the time to deny yourself the things that make you happy with the intention of being able to feel happy in the absence of these things.

"Happiness is a state of mind."

Part II

2: High on Happiness

Basis:
- Acknowledge the full extent of the happiness you feel from each item previously listed.
- Learn how to summon feelings of happiness and joy that these items give you without physically possessing the items.
- Learn how to convert negative emotions into feelings of happiness through physical actions.
- Learn how to instantly find happiness at any time by becoming aware of gratitude.

IDEOLOGY

As I previously mentioned in this guide, the majority of people see happiness as a feeling they get from something or someone. You hear people say, "I'm not feeling happy" or "I just want to feel happy" or "This makes me feel happy". We attribute this form of high to the happiness we feel inside. If life is about a bunch of feelings, then why is it that people put so much value in the thing or object itself instead of the feeling it gives you? In reality, we as a people aren't paying for a feeling, experience or relationship. We are paying for the emotion or feeling that a certain item or experiences gives us. In retrospect the item or experience doesn't possess the feeling at all; it is simply a catalyst to help us summon these feelings that lie dormant within us. Human beings have spent several lifetimes trying to study the minds of all of God's living, conscious creatures. For some there is no replacement for the feeling you get when a dog runs towards you as soon as you

walk in the door from a long day of hard work. The wagging of the tail, and the jumping and running around at the excitement of your entrance, is all a part of the dog expressing its internal happiness. You entering the room is just the event the dog relates to as something that causes it to become ecstatic. So, we must realize we humans aren't the only species that has this gift of happiness stored in us. Once we fully understand that our creator has endowed every conscious living creature with this superpower, we will then be able to learn how to tap into these powers and summon them at will. All of the actions that go on outside of you are received by your mind and eyes to help you identify the actions, people or experiences that make you feel happy. In the same way, you can focus your mind completing actions that can bring you feeling of happiness by altering the biochemistry within in your own body.
Understanding how to be constantly be high on happiness requires first understanding that you control your happiness at all times., whether that be mentally, physically, or emotionally.

Step 2: High on Happiness

-With the items listed in Step 1, concentrate on the exact feeling of happiness those things or people give you. (This should be done in a meditative state for at least 30 seconds each. Use a stopwatch or alarm if needed.)

_____

_____

_____

_____

_____

* Purpose: By being able to concentrate on the feeling of happiness you associate with these items, you will be able to lock this feeling in your subconscious so you can use it at any time without having that item or person to be the cause.

-Think of the items listed in Step 1 as your antidote to any negative emotions you may have, but only as a temporary fix. With this in mind, write down all the ways you believe you can get the feeling these "antidotes" give you without actually using them.

_____

_____

_____

_____

_____

_____

_____

* Purpose: By doing this you are allowing yourself to be honest and aware of what you think gives you a feeling of happiness, while also admitting that these feelings can be ever-changing because they are caused by external conditions. Finding more in-depth solutions for your solutions gives you the power to rely on internal solutions instead of external solutions. The key is to live by means of the internal, which ensures longevity.

-Concentrate on memories and actions that give you some form of sadness or anger, then smile while thinking of these things.

(Hold your smile for at least 10 seconds)

_____

_____

_____

_____

_____

* Purpose: By doing this you can reverse how your mind and subconscious relates to bad thoughts, feelings and events. You will consciously reverse the biological and mental effect the idea, event or feeling has on your body and mind by smiling. **(Laughing or singing is also helpful)**

-Think of as many things as you can that you consider yourself to be grateful for.

_____

_____

_____

(Take a maximum of 20 seconds.)

* Purpose: Gratitude is the new happiness. Being grateful will help change your paradigm for any situation. Gratitude will allow you to not only see the happiness associated with any item or relationship you have, but it also allows you to not tie your happiness to a single object or person. The feeling of sadness that comes from the lack of an item or person comes from the act of attachment, but once you imbue the feeling or perspective with gratitude, your mind will allow you to see all levels of that item to be the cause for some level of happiness. Gratitude is the gateway to happiness. Instead of relinquishing your happiness to items outside of yourself, if you keep gratitude in mind, you will always have something within you to be grateful for. That will in turn cause you to see happiness in all situations.

Keys to Remember: High on Happiness

- The feeling of happiness that you relate to something can be summoned at any moment by meditating on the overall feeling those items, people or places give you.

- You can control your negative emotional states by changing your body's physical state- for example, by smiling, joyfully singing, laughing, sitting up straight or engaging in slow, deep breathing.

- By acknowledging what you are grateful for, you can instantly summon a feeling of happiness from within by concentrating on what you currently possess in your life.

- When you are in a mental state of happiness you will attract more of what you want and less of what you don't want through a vibrational match.

- The perspective you have toward happiness will greatly influence how easily you can tap into the positive energy that comes with being happy. You are able to be constantly high on happiness once you train your mind to find happiness in everything that happens to you.

"When I'm grateful it becomes easier for me to see the happiness within my situations."

Part III

3. Own Your Happy

Basis:
- Identify and analyze all the items you listed in the previous sections.
- Evaluate how each item relates to controlling and/or owning your level of happiness.
- Recognize the overall effect that each item has on your level of happiness.
- Devise and implement plans to help assist in controlling full ownership of your happiness.

IDEOLOGY

As a society we tend to place our happiness in things or people that are outside of ourselves. We take the things or people we relate our happiness to and grant them the responsibility of controlling our happiness. Once we do this, we instantly relinquish the power to own our happiness. The idea that happiness comes from something or someone else is the major cause for people's lack of happiness or "happy currency".

You must ask yourself what state of being you were in prior to obtaining that object or meeting that person. Do you think your emotional or mental state was consistent with what you felt after meeting that person or acquiring that object? Your happiness is yours and can only dwindle if you allow yourself to give it away. It's no one's responsibility but your own to manage your level of happiness.

When you purchase a car that you spent your hard-earned money to buy and it gets dirty, you don't blame your kids or friends for the condition in which the car is kept. So, what sense would it make to blame someone or something for not giving you the happiness that you already possess inside? It doesn't make any logical sense to make someone feel obligated to give you what you already own from within. The biggest mistake we make is blaming other people or objects for our lack of happiness. Knowing that you fully own and control your happiness allows you to dictate to whom you lend your happiness. By understanding this you will never be caught thinking that someone can deplete you of your own happiness.

The next time someone is in your presence, monitor the level of happiness that you have while being in their company. This will give you great insight into if you're in complete control of your happiness or are you easily manipulated by your surroundings. The power in owning your happiness will set you on the right path to having your happiness. No longer will you feel drained or deprived of your happiness after engaging with someone or in a certain activity. Take control of your life by taking ownership of your happiness.

Step 3: Own Your Happy

- Refer to the previous list you made of the things and/or *people* that you think make you happy.

_____

_____

_____

_____

_____

* Purpose: To create a list of items or people that may own your happiness. Having a written list gives you a visual of the things, people or actions that you may think you connect the feeling of happiness to.

- Mentally imagine removing yourself from these things as a source of happiness.

_____

_____

_____

_____

_____

.

* Purpose: By removing these items as a source of happiness, you will regain ownership of your happiness and no longer place the power of it in anything outside of yourself and your control.

- Before you engage in any action that you think will make you happy, consider if your level of happiness will be affected by the presence, outcome or lack thereof this activity.

_____

_____

_____

_____

_____

* Purpose: When you can look ahead to see if your level of happiness will be affected by something, you will gain the ability to determine how much of yourself you want to expend on an action, event or person. You must be aware that happiness is energy and can be replenished or diminished as a form of currency. (We will discuss this in further detail in Part 4 of this book)

- Meditate on the list of things you think give you happiness and say "My happiness is mine. My happiness is not in_____." (Insert an item from the list.)

_____

_____

_____

_____

_____

*Purpose: This will give you a physical option and action that will help you regain and own your happiness.

- Think of anything that you may give your happiness to and may cause you to have a negative feeling like anger, sickness or frustration.

_____

_____

_____

_____

_____

*Purpose: You will gain more insight into what you allow to interfere with your happiness.

- With those negative thoughts and events, say, "These actions, feelings or events will not take or control my happiness."

_____

_____

_____

_____

_____

* Purpose: By speaking to your mind and subconscious, you give yourself more opportunities to free your happiness from being confined by certain actions, events or feelings. By doing this you will feel a sense of freedom about where you place your happiness and joy. Saying and believing this truth will give you the power you need to shift your perspective during times of discouragement, sadness and confusion.

Keys to Remember: Own Your Happy

- Being aware of what you think controls your mood allows you to dictate if these items will continue to have power over your feelings of happiness.

- Before engaging in an action or with a person, ask yourself if your happiness will be compromised by it.

- Always keep in mind the items or people that you think make you happy, so you can be more aware of where your happiness is being distributed.

- You have the power to detach yourself from any idea, item or person that you believe has the power to affect your happiness.

- You must acknowledge but never dwell on those actions, people or things that cause you to feel negative emotions.

"My happiness is mine."

PART IV

4. Rich in Happiness

Basis:
- Learn how to implement more positive activities that encourage feelings of happiness in your life.
- Understand the importance of happiness being measured as a form of currency that can be used as emotional leverage.
- Learn to expend your energy accordingly to prevent overexertion on things, people and actions that don't encourage feelings of happiness and positivity.
- Acknowledge the usage of gratitude and how it can be a catalyst to increase the amount of 'happy currency" you possess in your life.
- Learn to call upon happy memories to help reinforce your reserve of "happy currency", so that it may be useful for you in times of sadness, anger, frustration etc.

IDEOLOGY

We go to work and do all types of task with hope that it will bring us some form of monetary value. We see money as the driving force in everyone's life. "Can't live without it," is what most will say. If you are working to make money so that you are able to purchase the items that make you happy, then why wouldn't concentrate on being in a healthy state of mind that allows you to work at your peak performance?

In order to perform at your highest level, you must have some form of motivation from within. Most people are motivated by the feelings they think an item or person will give them. When you learn to be rich in happiness, you become capable of extracting the happiness out of anything and everything. The person that is rich in "happy currency" can see the positive side in everything, not because that thing or person makes them happy but because they are happy with or without that person or thing. Learn to become abundant in happiness and it will help you acquire all the monetary riches you desire.

STEP 4: Rich in Happiness

- Concentrate on increasing the amount of positive and healthy activities in your life. Relate all these activities to a form of happiness that is not temporary or instant gratification but more of a long-term feeling of joy and fulfillment.

_____

_____

_____

_____

_____

* Purpose: Knowing the activities that really bring out a long-lasting feeling of happiness in your life will help you eliminate the activities that don't help you summon beneficial, lasting happiness. By doing this you will be fully aware of where and what to spend your "happy currency" on.

- Be conscious and aware of the emotions you spend your energy on. With each task, action or thing you do, try to consciously think of how much of your "happy currency" will be expensed for the sake of these actions.

_____

_____

_____

_____

_____

_____

* Purpose: This will help you evaluate the worth of each emotion you have in your life and the energy you apply to them. By practicing this you will eventually realize what emotions or feelings are worth spending your energy on and compromising your "happy currency". If practiced consistently you will come to the conclusion that no emotion should be within you long enough that it starts to deplete your "happy currency". The point in being rich in happiness is to not dismiss the other emotions, but to bring awareness to how powerful "happy currency" is in comparison to all other feelings, emotions and/or states of mind.

- Use the items listed as things you're grateful for to be your reservoir from where you pull your feelings of happiness. The longer the list of things you have to be grateful for, the more "happy currency" you have reserved. Picture gratitude as the labor or work you apply to be compensated for in happiness.

_____

_____

_____

_____

_____

* Purpose: Using gratitude as the catalyst to get your feelings of happiness going makes it easier for you to curb any negative or detrimental feelings by changing your state of mind from something negative to something positive. The idea is to keep your "happy currency" reserve as high as possible so it may serve you in future days when most needed. This is easily accomplished by having several things you are grateful for and can call upon in times of despair.

Keys to Remember: Rich in Happiness

- Happy actions create happy feelings, you must manifest your happiness through what you do on an everyday basis.

- Engage in activities that bring you happiness that is lasting, not just for instant gratification.

- People who surround themselves with happy people tend to be happier, and in the same sense happy people tend to attract happy people.

- Focus on reserving your energy during certain engagements that may cause you to feel drained.

- Use whatever you consider to be grateful for in life as a source for your happiness. It is important to have these in mind during times of discouragement or sadness.

- Be aware of how much energy you expend for the sake of an emotion. The energy spent on negative emotions can be reserved for feelings of happiness.

- Your "happy currency" is the true value that will help you obtain all your monetary desires, so be aware of how you spend it.

"Happy is the new wealthy."

PART V

5. Speak Happiness, Hear Happiness

Basis:
- Establish firm affirmations that will help you build a strong mental foundation through your subconscious.
- Practice the daily usage of mantras to help reinforce your belief in the ideals that bring you happiness.
- Provide yourself with easily accessible affirmations, quotes and mantras that can be used in times of need.

IDEOLOGY

These affirmations, quotes and mantras are meant to be used at any time you see fit. Its best to look over them at least once daily. The true power in affirmations is the faith and belief you have after you speak them out into the universe. The affirmation is useless and is a waste of energy and time to the nonbeliever.

Whether people realize it or not, they are speaking affirmations into existence. And the most detrimental part about it is that most people affirm things that they truly do not believe or want to receive. Any thought, word or idea that is manifested with extreme emotion will surely come to fruition due to the strong magnetic force that emotions have within.

That is why it is of utmost importance that you understand why affirming happiness in your life is the greatest force to have and be rich in. Your subconscious does not know the difference between jokes and seriousness. It does not know whether you really meant something or not.

So, I advise you to feed your subconscious beneficial truths that will help serve your life's purpose in the greatest way. Use these affirmations, quotes and mantras as if they were part of your everyday routine and watch how drastically your life changes. Once consistently practiced you will truly become rich in the "happy currency".

- Listed are a few affirmations, quotes and mantras that will help keep you conscious of owning and being rich in happiness.

STEP 5: Speak Happiness Hear Happiness

- "My happiness is mine."

- "My happiness is not in_____.

- "These actions, feelings and/or events will not take or control my happiness."

- "Happiness is a state of mind."

- "Gratitude is the new happiness."

- "Happiness is within me, so happiness is all I will give."

- "No matter what is given to me, I will find happiness within it."

- "I am as happy as I tell myself I am."

- "I will never allow something outside of me to control my level of happiness."

- "Happy people live longer."

- "The things I tell myself can influence my level of happiness. I will tell myself only things that will bring happiness out of me."

- "When I am grateful it becomes easier for me to see happiness within my situations."

- "How happy I am, have been, and will be is determined by the way my mind perceives life."

- "It takes the same amount of energy to be happy as it does to be sad."

- "When you are happy you are helpful to all those around you."

- "When you place your happiness in something outside of yourself, you increase the chances of that something being able to run off with your happiness."

- "Happy is the new wealthy."

- "A happy person has too much to be happy for, which leaves them no room to be hateful towards anything or anyone."

- "I have all the happiness I will ever need within in me right now."

- "Searching for happiness outside of yourself is like a fish searching for water to breathe in the desert. It will find more within itself than it does in its surroundings."

- "Happiness is in the head."

Keys to Remember: Speak Happiness, Hear Happiness

- Affirmations must be spoken with firm belief or they have no value in your life.

- You must feel the results you are looking for from the affirmations, quotes and mantras while you say them. If happiness is what you're expecting to get from saying them, then you must think of happiness while saying them.

- All of these quotes can be spoken throughout the day, but they are most effective if done when you first wake up and right before you go to sleep.

- It is best to say the affirmations once a day the first week then once a week from then on to give your subconscious some time to absorb and put to use the words within the affirmations.

- Once spoken enough, its best to not speak affirmations, quotes or mantras but instead just meditate on them

"I am as happy as I tell myself I am."

CONCLUSION

Whether it means how you feel, how you live or even how you act, the idea of happiness can vary for everyone. Most people spend their whole life trying to figure out what happiness truly means to them. Throughout history, humans have pursued happiness by means of money, power, sex, drugs and their livelihoods. Families have been broken up due to the lack of happiness in the relationship that the family was founded upon.

For years society has always encouraged people to find happiness in something that dwells outside of themselves. The media continues to give people false hope that their one product above all others is the key to the happiness that everyone is seeking. For far too long we have given up the ownership of our happiness and have not only become financially stricken but poor in happiness as well.

When you go out, you see a world full of material things that hold no true spiritual value and reward when it comes to having a long-lasting happiness. With this short guide to owning your happiness and being rich in the "happy currency", I bestow light upon a dark path which will aid you on the journey to finding your happiness. The purpose of this guide is to make sure you never have to look outside of your own mind, spirit and heart to find the happiness that every human covets and deserves. When you feel like you are detouring from the path, refer to this guide to give you a sense of direction and clarity. Whenever your days start to overwhelm you, refer to this guide to always remember that "Your Happiness is Yours."

BLANK SPACE FOR NOTES

www.ingramcontent.com/pod-product-compliance
Lightning Source LLC
Chambersburg PA
CBHW072209100526
44589CB00015B/2446